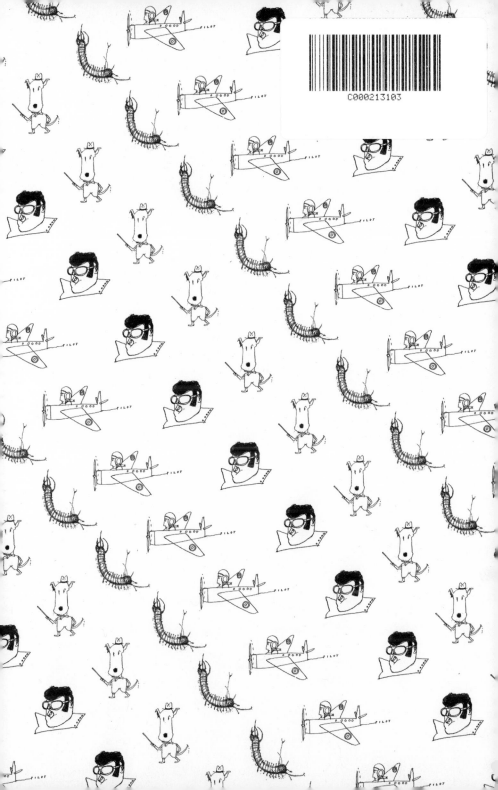

WHERE EARWIGS DARE

MATT HARVEY

green books

Acknowledgements

I am grateful once again to David Hughes, whose brilliant illustrations adorn the outside and mid-section of this book. I'll be very happy if people judge the book by its cover.

Many of these poems appeared in the 'Work' section of *The Guardian*, and I'd like to thank my editors Ian Wylie – who first invited me to write the Desktop Poetry slot – and Graham Snowdon. Several were first heard on BBC Radio 4's Saturday Live, so I'd also like to say a warm thank you to the Saturday Live team past and present, especially Becky Vincent, Maria Williams, Lottie Barker, Debbie Kilbride, JP Devlin, Simon Clancy, Maggie Olgiati, Rev Richard Coles and Fi Glover.

Oh Potato and *Bread* were commissioned by the Waste and Resources Action Project (WRAP) for its 'Love Food Hate Waste' campaign. *Less is More* was written for, and at, the Schumacher Conference of the same name in 2008. *Cloud appreciation* and *If I said you had a bit of a problem would you hold it against me?* first appeared in the *Commonhead* anthology published by Blue Gate Books. A handful of these verses appeared originally in one or more of the self-published chapbooks *Here We Are Then, Songs Sung Sideways, Standing Up to be Counted Out* and *Curtains and Other Material*. *Two-way Domestic Totnestic Acrostic* was commissioned by *The Independent*.

Invaluable sounding-board services were provided variously by my wife, Heather; my parents, Tim and Sheila Harvey; and by Phil Rigg, Naomi Jaffa, Dean Parkin, Lynne Gerlach and Amanda Williamson. I would also like to acknowledge and thank my sons, Finn and Tom, for their love of rhyming language and brutally accurate impersonations of performance poets.

Finally, I would like to thank everyone at Green Books for their warm welcome and enthusiasm, in particular Amanda Cuthbert, whose notion this was and who followed through with tremendous tenacity and tact!

Also by Matt Harvey and illustrated by David Hughes: *The Hole in the Sum of My Parts*, published by The Poetry Trust, and, for children, *Shopping With Dad*, illustrated by Miriam Latimer and published by Barefoot Books.

Published in 2010 by Green Books, Foxhole, Dartington, Totnes, Devon TQ9 6EB

Text © Matt Harvey 2010
Illustrations © David Hughes 2010

All rights reserved

Design inspired by Jack Pearce and Rob Steer of Silk Pearce, who designed *The Hole in the Sum of My Parts*

Text printed on 100% recycled paper (Corona Natural, with centre section on Five Seasons Book-White). Printed in the UK by TJ International, Padstow, Cornwall.

ISBN 978 1 900322 87 4

To my Mum and Dad

CONTENTS

SLUG

low-born land mollusc
high-impact intruder
easy oozer, slime exuder
free-loader, sprout-spoiler
meandering marauder
disrespecter
of my broad beans' border
you've a one-track mind
in a one-track body

diligent pillager
soft-horned invisigoth
slow silver scribbler
paradoxically busy sloth
tithe-taker, hole-maker
indiscriminate direct debitor
bold-as-brass brassica editor

you're a squishetty spoilsport
a glistening drag
the liquorice allsort
nobody wants to find in the bag

it's time that you were brought to book
you're not as tasty as you look
listen chum, you are disposable
look at my thumb, it is opposable

unwelcome invertebrate
this might just hurt a bit
I pluck you and chuck you
into distant dew-drenched greenery
isn't that mean of me?

slug, when all is said and done
you can hide but you can't run

THE COMPANY OF LEEKS

down through the generations
we've been generating leeks
we've not won *all* the prizes
but we've had our winning streaks
won enough to furnish houses –
we've had fewer troughs than peaks
in the company of leeks

rosettes, I've had a few
and then some honourable mentions
to see a leek you, yourself, grew
receiving plaudits and attention
when that leek in peak condition
wins a Best Leek Competition
you feel so cock-a-hoop
it calls for cock-a-leekie soup
although it isn't Mum's leek pudding
…it'll do

for what is a leek – what is it like?
let's take a look – let's sneak a peek
a cylinder of bundled sheafs
tortilla wrap of Welsh motifs
a spring onion on steroids
or – roots on – pagan Barbie
close relation of the onion
upside-down Olympic flame
they are Garlic's kissing cousin
they're an eco-party-popper in freeze-frame

a little bit ineffable
a heavy-metal daffodil
it makes me feels so affable
the company of leeks

so you can keep your Spanish beach
I'll stay where leeks are within reach
 – the tasty part of vichyssoise –
and while the world around me sleeps
beneath the undemanding stars
I'll keep the company of leeks

CLOUD APPRECIATION

clouds – what are you like?
drizzly drifters, shapely shifters
unfitted fixtures, thumbless hitchers
3D thought bubbles
congealed whispers
sky putty, atmospheric play dough,
free range shaving foam,
fish impersonators
huff puff chuff chuff buffer zones
ghost modernists, God's pocket fluff
angel plops
ectoplasm with altitude, séance stuff
ozone bolstery, heavenly upholstery
stuffing with nothing to be knocked out of
weather workers, rain dispensers, farmer charmers
extremists
condensation culture
cream of nothingness soup with aeroplane croutons
airy nothings claiming their right of assembly
inefficient strobe lighting
non-dairy crème fraîche
shamanic sheep shearings
scatter meringues
how now, sky cow?
you'll be the rumination of me…

clouds
your proliferation
is appreciated

A WATCHED CLOCK

To think that time, of all things, can be managed
as if a team or medical condition,
and not the yester-moment, ever-vanished –
lift-music, teacher, healer and beautician.
Pick up an old saw. If you need to, tweak it.
Pull fingers out, socks up, and get your skates on.
Sow something. Great. Wait for it, wait, wait… Reap it!
A million cliché-users can't be wrong.
Time heals all wounds and yet it gives no quarter.
Time flies, and yet takes longer than you think
to lead the horse you changed mid-stream to water.
A watched clock never boils, unless you blink.
The early bird catches the worm, it's said –
that's why the wise worm turns and stays in bed.

STREAKER

jiggly jokery
giggley blokery
he's an artful jammy dodger
with a bibbly bobbly todger

it's a wanton bit of wobbling
spontaneous life-modelling
a cheeky breach of protocol
a unilateral photo call

it reminds us we are humans
it's a chance to use your zoom lens
there's a curious catharsis as
they put the 'arse' in narcissist

but it isn't for the insecure
and nor for the incontinent
you really have to be cocksure
thick-skinned and ultra-confident

so don't streak if you're peaky
or recovering from surgery
or if your nooks and crannies
have a fair degree of verdigris

don't streak if you're angry
it's important to be dangly

streaking through a nudist camp
is technically just jogging
(but if you put your togs back on
you're what's known as a streaking Tom)

never streak near welding gear
or churches, mosques or synagogues
never do it anywhere
you think there might be sniffer dogs

but once you've streaked at Aintree
the Tour de France and Barcelona
worn your birthday suit at Ascot
and the Bull Run at Pamplona
done double-faults at Wimbledon
before Miss Kournikova
you must begin to think
perhaps your hobby's taking over

and maybe you have crossed that subtle line
between waving your organ of intimacy
and simply being one

THE FULL EMPATHIC MILE

To walk a mile in someone else's shoes,
to look out from behind their eyes, to feel
how they might feel, and know why they might choose
to cross the line – to hurt, to cheat, to steal.

To wear rogues' brogues, a mugger's mules, a stalker's sneakers
an embezzler's espadrilles, crack-dealers' clogs
an industrial polluter's winkle-pickers –
to be empathic is to walk thus shod.

We could go further on the cat-walk of compassion
try socks, skirts, slacks, assorted leisure wear.
Beneath the beige we'll sense the treasure there
though it may not be the cutting edge of fashion.

Let's not let such idealism be scorned
or shrugged off with a patronising smile.
But remember – walk the full empathic mile,
and not a merely metric one. Be warned:

I'm speaking now with hindsight and with candour
of the time when I tried on my sister's bra
then felt self-conscious and did not walk far –

and to this day I still don't understand her…

THROUGH A GLASS HARDLY

Why is my career stalling?
Have my standards somehow fallen,
others' standards quietly lifted?
Have the magic goalposts shifted?
Am I such an awful ogress?
What could block my upward progress?

Am I simply out of touch?
Too feminine, too butch, too much?
Have I been too soft and silent,
other times too strong and strident?
Too supine, sanguine, bovine, ursine?
Candidly – is it my star sign?

Is my ego growing swollen?
Have I misused a semicolon?
Thought too far outside the box?
Sworn too freely, worn odd socks?
Be honest. Are there any clues?
Is it my attitude? These shoes?

Is my clothing too revealing?
Or, by contrast, too concealing?
Do I need, you know, *enhancement*
to procure career advancement?
Is it… hygiene? You can tell me.
Have a quick sniff. Go on, smell me!

What makes me so unappealing?
What *about* the bloody ceiling?
It's glass? So what?
It's… Oh. I see.
Right.
Okay, well, in that case…
   anyone fancy a nice cup of tea?

EMPATH MAN

This scene is an introduction to contemporary superhero Empath Man, who fights crime with his advanced listening skills and ability to stay open and vulnerable in a tight situation.

Warehouse. Interior. Two desperate men, stuffing wads of cash into a duffel bag, look up, startled, as a man strolls casually through the double doors...

"Hi guys, looks like fun. Guess you must need the money pretty bad. Hey – I've been there. I know where you're coming from."

"Oh no, it's Empath Man! Don't let him disarm you with his self-deprecating charm and non-judgemental acceptance of who you are."

"I guess you must have felt quite an emptiness inside to need to fill it with bundles of cash. It's as if that duffel bag is your crumpled, deprived heart and this is an honest but confused attempt to meet its needs. I respect that. I find it moving."

"Damn you, Empath Man. I don't want to talk about this shit right now."

"Don't let him get to you. Shoot him if you have to."

"Hey, if you need to shoot me, I guess you need to shoot me. I feel very open and accepting of who you are and what you do."

"Shoot him!"

"I can't."

"Can't or won't?"

"I dunno, part of me wants to shoot him, another part just wants to relax and hang out with the guy. The mixture of serenity and sheer ordinariness is strangely compelling..."

"OK. Give me the gun. I'll shoot him myself."

"Hey," Empath Man shrugs. "Whatever you need to do, you know, that's okay. Trust yourself. Who else can you trust? Who else have you ever been able to trust?"

"Goddamn it, I'm filling up!"

"What's he doing to you, Rodney, what's happening?"

"I don't know. It's this talk of trust. It's bringing up long-buried feelings."

"Long-buried what?"

"Feelings."

"Goddamn. You've got to fight it."

"I'm trying, it's just… they've been buried so long beneath encrusted layers of anger and cynicism, wrapped around in bravado and self-medication, it's kind of a big thing for me."

The soft man keeps talking. "What feelings are coming up? It's just me and your partner in crime here. You can tell us."

"Feelings of hurt, sadness, loss, betrayal, and, Oh God, no…"

"What is it? We both want to hear it."

"A kind of self-loathing, a sense of shame, allied with a yearning of almost spiritual intensity."

"No, please, don't go spiritually intense on me now. I'm feeling pretty shaky as it is. Don't… Oh God, it's the Police."

Screech of tyres, slam of doors, pounding of meaty feet. It's Karma in a uniform. Empath Man keeps eye contact with the overwrought robber as he greets the men in blue.

"Hello Officers, these two miscreants here were just opening up to some feelings about crime and the causes of crime, I'm sure they'll be more than willing to carry on down at the station."

The two are roughly cuffed and led away. "Come on then, miscreants, and stop snivelling, or we'll really give you something to cry about down at the cells."

"Hmmm. We all feel the desire to brutally punish others in order to bolster our own diminished sense of personal power."

"That's enough, Empath Man. I've got to hand it to you, another job well done. But I don't like your methods. They're effective, but they're sick."

"I understand, Officer, what it is to be both disgusted and threatened by emotional intensity and authentic intimacy. I too have insecurities gnawing at me like ravenous rats devouring the living tissue of self-worth. But thanks for the feedback. I'll take it on board – even though it may corrode my soul like the acid of early rejection by a parent or carer. But hey, I'm sensing you'd know about that."

The officer turns away. Are those tears welling up? Probably.

As usual, Empath Man is left alone to reflect. He wasn't always Empath Man – used to be just a regular guy, in middle management. Then he took part in a drugs trial that went horribly wrong. It was an anti-pessimism drug, Optiagra. For middle-aged men who find it difficult to get their hopes up.

He had a wife, Stella. She was always trying to get him to see a Relate counsellor with her, but he wasn't having any of that. When he became Empath Man Stella was like the cat who got the cream – then became lactose-intolerant on the same day. Because who could live with such a man – in whose presence all feeling is amplified; who knows how you feel before you do; who brings out the best in you at the worst possible time?

So here we leave him, the Skinless Wonder, the Lone Listener, putting the vigil back in vigilante...

THINK BEFORE YOU PRINT THIS POEM

made entirely from offcuts and recycled popular hits,
hand-stitched non-seamlessly together

to see a hot tub in a council skip
and heaven in a bald tyre
behold infinity in your local tip
and eternity in some frayed electrical wire

it seems one man's chimney pot's another man's top hat
one man's bauble is another man's jewel
one man's cheapskate's another man's skip-rat
one man's chip fat's another man's fuel
one man's cheek is another man's chutzpah
one man's puddle is another man's foot spa

broken umbrellas, malfunctioning kettles
empty containers of various metals
that never quite did what it said on their tins
these are a few of my favourite things

and one man's tip is another man's temple
one man's junk is another man's joy
one man's meat is another man's pen pal
one man's man is another girl's boy
one man's popgun's another man's uzi
one man's grit is another man's muesli

leftovers, hand-me-downs, chuckaways, offcuts
used, pre-loved, second-hand, rejects and cast-offs
all the fresh junk that this rampantly unsustainable consumer society
                                                                    brings
these are yet more of my favourite things

when the cold bites, when my skip leaks
    when I've lost my zest
I simply dismember my favourite things
    and then I don't feel so stressed

FOOTPRINTS

I searched for metric meanings
along the grinding beach,
but despite my mystic leanings
they were always out of reach.

I dug for deeper answers
beneath the padded sands,
but all I found were dancers
with seaweed on their hands.

Though I boned up on the history
and strove to keep the score,
the sea remained a mystery
and I remained ashore.

Still I'd seek to know the essence
of what I am today,
for the proof of my pale presence
will soon be washed away,

and the seedbed of my questions
will be covered by the sea,
where my bones shall find a rest home
when I'm no longer me.

Though I remember all the faces
and record what I have seen
the sea will wash away the traces
as though they'd never been.

For the sea's here to remind us
as we walk upon the land
that all we leave behind us
are footprints in the sand.

And footprints in the sand, it's said,
however deep and wide,
will not keep their distinctive tread
beyond the next high tide.

We pay ourselves such compliments
yet barely understand
the greatest of our monuments
are footprints in the sand.

THE INNOCENT EVERYDAY OCEAN

many's the many who haven't a penny
    and too are the few who speak true
and sore is the rawness of people whose poorness
    discolours the deeds that they do

for hurly the burly that wakes us so early
    and puts us to bed when it's late
and gravy the train that we're riding in vain
    till the pattern is licked off our plate

fleeced are the flock that live chock upon block
    and jowl by bowel to boot
while they're licking their lips over fat fish and chips
    someone's picking the lock of their loot

and thin are the thinkers who walk round in blinkers
    and etched is the stretch of their smile
singing "Such is the suchness of all of our muchness
    that wide is the width of our while"

unruffled the feathers of bikers in leathers
    and roughshod their ticket to ride
while sunbathers toil beneath lashings of oil
    until tastefully tanned is their hide

unchecked are the jackets of punters in packets
    and snide is the back of their stab
and tongue-tied the twisters who give themselves blisters
    so glib is the gift of their gab

unhitched are the hikers who think they don't like us
    the more we drive past in our cars
there's always a catch or an itch you can't scratch
    like a haemorrhoid far up your arse

and pearly the gates where the Lord Jesus waits
    with his merciful scales in his hand
if you're caught in arrears then he'll wipe off your tears
    and he'll set you down safe on dry land

a sign in the suburb said "Do not disturb
    while our daughters are trying to diet
there's a hard garden gnome standing guard on our home
    and he'll kill for some peace and some quiet"

a man with a mangle has found a new angle
    he's set up a new scene to steal
when he gets to the bank he knows just who to thank
    but he's fallen asleep at the wheel

a young woman curses and clicks shut her purse as
    the Good Shepherd shuts up his shop
she married a butcher who sawed off her future
    then came home and gave her the chop

she knew what to do for her dreams to come true
    but she got off to such a false start
while the young man was fishing for the price of admission
    she was hoping to hump off his heart

you win some you lose some you grow a big tum
    where there may be a baby inside
when it enters the world be it boy beast or girl
    it's got nothing whatever to hide

so we send it to schools where they ram home the rules
    with an iron hand in a kid glove
sweet voices of reason speak words of pure treason
    to sandwich the language of love

so harmless the gormless whose thoughts are so formless
	our jawbones hang open in shame
we're taught to wear nylon and hats with a smile on
	to labour, lay bets and lay blame

and humpty the dumpty whose life is so empty
	he spends all his days on a wall
there's nothing inside but his terrible pride
	to come between him and his fall

his albumen's thick as a liquefied brick
	and he'll tell you the outlook is grim
his razor-blade laugh can near cut you in half
	but he knows that the yoke is on him

while cross-legged commuters caress their computers
	(so mild are their manners and meek)
torrential the tears that run down our careers
	until blub is the chub of our cheek

and staid are the stable who do what they're able
	precise, to the point are their prayers
and crazy the paving of those who are slaving
	or drowning by numbers in pairs

and sung is the song of the sad and the simple
	and dug is the ditch of their deep
and soft are the screams that encircle our dreams
	so sound is the snug of our sleep
		our sleep
	and sound is the snug of our sleep

ABOUT A BEE

with a low matchmaking murmur
from bloom to bloom fumble with fervour
the honeybees

we owe them
but let's not assume
we know them

for we project on to the bee
utopian society
their attitude, their industry
the bee's seen as exemplary

I'll quarrel with the moralists
the bee to me
is seasonal accessory
nature's necessity

honey maker, pollen picker
stamen shaker, pistil licker
floating voter
stigma stroker
window basher, private dancer
picnic crasher, lip enhancer

black-and-yeller hive dweller
anaphylaxis point of access

unexpected aviator, blind dater, pollinator
distant lawnmower impersonator

metaphor provider, inflorescence inspector
hairdo inspirer, nectar collector

these things and more are what make me
make much ado about a bee

WATER-COOLER MOMENTS

we shared water-cooler moments
every other other day
wishful water-cooler moments
and they can't take them away
wry, dry looks that had no witnesses
rueful smiles and knowing grimaces
I can't prove it, but we shared them
and I like to think you cared then
that you weren't just being nice to me
you sent memos with your eyes to me
and I reciprocated
though I may have mistranslated
meanings added, meanings missed
I'm pretty sure I got the gist

we didn't ever action
our unminuted attraction
we each knew that we shouldn't
so we didn't, though we could, it
seemed we had an understanding
or that's how I understood it
till that moment when you winced at me
went halfway to convincing me
I'd passed the out-of-order-line
and hovered on the borderline
between being an embarrassment
and being charged with harassment
and then you merged with Marketing

and now to my intense regret
you use the little kitchenette
that's time-shared with the second floor
a long mile down the corridor
the rest's not even history
there never was a you and me
though might have been so easily

there's a question that's implicit here
and I admit I'm begging it –
okay, the word 'relationship'
pudding-wise, is over-egging it
Re: 'the first stone' let those who've never
wished and wondered cast it –
it was a beautiful speculationship
while it lasted

SILENCE OF THE DOMINOES

what's that sound? it's so unsettling
I think you'd better put the kettle on

you can call us coots and geezers
codgers, biddies, hags and wheezers
give us Murray mints and Mintoes
when we asked you for Maltesers

but we're the comeback generation
we're confounding expectation
that we stay home with our succulents
no we're not on medication
we prefer to call them supplements

we're retiring from retirement
so good riddance to good riddance
it's no longer a requirement
acquiesce to being a pensioner?
it's the first step to dementia

though it might sound contradictory
we are old dogs with new trickery
we're shrugging off the stereotypes
though some of us *are* very old tykes
who do inhale Vicks Vapours
write broadsides to local papers
and say, "What's that in old money?"

but we've known our share of darker times
and no, these are not laughter-lines
– nothing's quite that funny –

yes our faces are more lived-in
– we're reflective, not defective –
and we don't do heavy lifting
and our hearing is selective

so what's that sound you find so ominous?
it's the silence of the dominoes…

BUBBLES

No bubble ever blown was built to last
indefinitely – all must burst some day –
Kaput. Finito. No elastoplast
or welding gear could make them last the day.
Since every bubble bears within the essence
of every other bubble ever blown,
and each is blessed with built-in obsolescence,
it's not improbable our very own
so-called Big Bang was just another bubble –
that which physicists assure us was the first
primeval impulse, root of all our trouble –
just a bubble in the void that simply burst.
Likewise when Time puts our world to a stop
we'll end, not with a bang, but with a POP!

THE AMAZING MEMORY MAN'S
MAGICAL MEMORIES

an unforgetful love poem

I remember the dress that you wore when we met
the dress with the dots – how could I forget
two hundred and four – none exactly the same
I counted them all as you came through the door
    …gave each one a name

we walked out together, beneath a lumpy grey sky
I see it so clearly now in my mind's eye
the pavement, the drizzle, the cars grumbling by…
    Ford Mondeo, blue, N76 RBT
    Toyota Corolla, white, C213 XPL
    Citroen Picasso, red, S79 YAE

You kissed me. I missed one. But I didn't mind.
We were young. We had time.

The restaurant. We held hands. Once more we kissed.
And whispered sweet nothings – well, you did,
I whispered the whole set menu and wine list –
(and what's really nice is:
 I can still recite it, including the prices)

and then back to your place, your face stuck to my face
while my eyes memorised your CDs
I noticed a book there beside the computer
the abridged Kama Sutra 'for the hurried lover'
in two minutes I'd read it – from cover to cover

you said, "Hey do you seriously think that kind of thing can impress me?"
and I closed the book, and my eyes, and said, "Test me…"

MY KIND OF TOWN

For some time now I've lived in Totnes, considered by some to be the capital of alternative Britain. Totnes has a soft, spiritually seeking, self-improving, green ambience. Even the water is very soft. When it emerges into the open sea it gets picked on by hard waters from other regions.

Alternative Technology
But I feel very comfortable here, probably because I'm into alternative technology, complementary medicine and cutting-edge psychotherapy. Recently I've been involved in a project to develop a car which runs entirely on suppressed rage. We started out with a scooter powered by anxiety, but this used to speed up when it came to a hazard, and we had our funding cut.

Godseeker's Allowance
Speaking of funding, the government has been experimenting with a pilot benefit scheme in Totnes. It is actually possible to claim Godseeker's Allowance. I signed on for it myself. They take it very seriously. You have to sign a form saying you're available for and actively seeking God, then you have to say whether you're prepared to travel, how far, and whether you're intending to travel externally in your search for God, or internally. I put down that I was searching internally, because it's very difficult to check. After three months you get called in for a Godsearch Review. They sit you down and say, "Well, it says here you've been searching for a nurturing, healing, redemptive God, but you haven't had much luck. Would you consider broadening your search to include a harsh, judgemental, punishing God…?" and of course if you say no they can cut your benefit.

Time

In Totnes people have time to talk, and even in small talk there's space for the big questions. Recently a foreign-language student approached me in the High Street and asked, "Excuse me please, uh, what is, uh, time?" I said, "I'm really glad you asked me that, because the fascinating but elusive question of the nature and meaning of time has fascinated thinkers since the earliest periods of philosophical enquiry. For some, time is 'of the essence'; for others, time is 'money'. For some the space/time dichotomy is analogous to the body/mind split, whilst for others this is bollocks.

"The ancient Greeks", I went on, "used to distinguish between Chronos, the passage of time, and Kairos, the experience of the passage of time, and at the Arcturus Float Centre in Totnes High Street you can get Chrono-Cairo-Colonic Irrigation, where they push a clear plastic tube up the passage of time and flush out faecal matter and historical detritus."

It sounds wacky I know, but I've tried it and ever since there just seem to be more hours in the day.

Hormones

Spending even a short time in Totnes can be relaxing and restoring. But when people have lived here for several years both men and women start to secrete the same hormone, Totnesterone, which balances the male and female principles in a pleasing yet practical way. It's lovely. It's my kind of town.

TWO-WAY DOMESTIC TOTNESTIC ACROSTIC*

Twinned with Glastonbury in your too-tender heart
Organic, outraged: "Say no to GMO!" "No!"
Tastefully tantric, not tacky – nothing like that
Natural, navel-gazing your own numinous abdomen
Empathic, embracing every ethical energy source
Sceptical of the non-existence of angels

* Notice how the poem spells Totnes down both the left- and right-hand side. If you study the text carefully you may eventually see the hidden pentagram embedded within – this spells out 'God is great. Buddha is terrific.' Some people claim to be able to see the distinctive spiral of DNA double-helix in the text, spelling out – against all known laws of probability – the phrase 'Professor Richard Dawkins is slightly over-confident.' Keep looking.

JAZZ GEOMETRY

sonnet celebrating the elegance, ingenuity and sheer cerebral power of Darren Crowdy's creative use of Schottky Groups to complete the Schwarz-Christoffel formula so that it works with irregular shapes and those with holes

You're clever, you. Far out. You're *way out there*
beyond the bozone layer where we reside,
you plot the line fantastic in the air
where Ancient Greek and Modern Geek collide.

You do Jazz Geometry – it can't be taught –
express yourself in dancing neuro-glyphs,
placing in brackets things that can't be taught
then multiplying by their absent widths.

You're out there where the holy grail or chalice is
where masthmatics like me can hardly breathe,
then with applied complex analysis
you bring it down to Earth – just for a wheeze.

You're far out. So far out. And so, so clever –
yet when you say *Eureka!* we say *Whatever…*

BENEDICTION

if evening came and clapped its hands
and no-one spoke and no-one wept
if silence stirred the rain-pocked sands
while high stars blinked and flesh stars slept

if agonies of space and time
contrive to heal a planet's core
and out of protoplasmic slime
a man articulates a roar

then no-one, dressed in words and rags
could circumnavigate the whole,
sum up its parts or down its dregs
disturb its peace or stain its soul

and everyone with silent grace
could turn their treadmill to the light
and show their true reflective face
restored to subtle sound and sight

let everyone who ever lived
who rose and fell without a trace
be privy to this simple gift
take pride in our divine disgrace

if briars blossom in the homes
of sun-tanned slaves of unmet need
if on their carpets sewage foams
and drowns the frail, untended seed

let children, mouthing sticks and stones
plant wheat and flowers on their graves
and sleep at night among our bones
with ancient fires to guard their caves

within whose shadows we might see
what might become of all of us
the people we would like to be
an essence which we hold in trust

a signpost stands where we once stood
and points the way to who we are
some singing of the Greater Good
some wishing on a savage star

we paw the pale, perplexing page
engraved with certainty and doubt
by those who strut the paper stage
who stand up to be counted out

we feed off our constituents
off fire and water, air and earth
and reel beneath their influence
from birth to death and death to birth

we cut our keys to fit our locks
and file them under Wrong and Right
we break like waves across the rocks
we wake like children in the night

THE WHOLE POTATO

I love the whole potato, skin and all,
the poe, the tay, the toe, it's criminal
to throw even a bit of it away
say, whoa! say hey! say whoa! hey whoa!
don't throw away the poe tay toe
do not betray the poe, the tay,
it's not the way to go, no way
you must be true to toe poe tay
to total poe and tay and toe,
the toe and tal of total too,
but not the be the tray the al
of betrayal – don't feed the crim
the in the all of criminal
but love the whole potato, skin and all

OH POTATO

no part of you's inedible – though all of you's inaudible
the taste of you's incredible – the price of you's affordable
no spud is dud – if you get sprouty
I don't go all throwy-outy
but focus all my passion
into peeling and to mashing
I still need you – so I freeze you –
saying softly, "see you later, mashed potater"

COWS

fat-flanked field furniture
wind-breakers, methane-makers
flatulence factories

flirty stop-outs, tectonic shifters
dew-lickers, weather predictors

voluminous ruminants, heft luggage
glazey-eyed space gazers
bovine buddhas

slumbery lumbering slobbery-gobs
rheumy-eyed tongue flollopers
twitch-tailed conductors of fly orchestras

biddable biddies, buttercup flatteners
popular-bottomed earth splatterers

cheese ancestry
solemnly sentient cereal processors
tragic disenfranchised McFood
beef on the bone in a bag

lowbrow meadow-sweeteners
foghorn impersonators
inarticulate mouthers of unfinished moon poetry

ROB THE RUBBISH

this is the title affectionately given to Robin Kevan, a retired social worker, in his home town of Llanwrtyd Wells, Powys, for voluntarily clearing litter from the town's streets each day

he isn't where the glamour is
or where the glitz and glitter is
he's far away from cameras
Rob is where the litter is
whose litter? ours!

sound citizens like me and you
who leave behind a residue
the wrapper of a snacky thing
petroleum-based packaging
an apple core, a bottle top
look! someone's dropped their glottal stop
the stray lid off some Tupperware
the forelock of a Sherpa there
a crushed carton of orange juice
the landscape soaks up this abuse

then Rob steps in
    and…
by picking up crisp packets, cling film and tinfoil
incongruous empties of Sprite and Drambuie
he nurtures the flora and fauna and topsoil
and subtly recharges the Feng of its Shui

Rob is more than merely stoic
he is verging on heroic
he's a super-dooper human
doing topographic grooming
here is a man whose civic pride
extends up every mountainside

he de-clutters their crevices
he's even done Ben Nevis's
the litter droppers' nemesis –
is he a hero? you decide

it's a dirty world – but Rob won't let us ruin it
it's a dirty job – we're glad that Rob is doing it

CUDDLING WITH HUMANS

though the thought of no more cuddling
is seriously troubling
when it comes to Cuddle Parties*
I admit that I am struggling

I may well be molly-coddled
in my own way jolly-muddled
and perhaps not fully-cuddled
but I get the collywobbles...
so if you think there's any chance I'll ever join the Cuddle Party –
I think, hardly

– I am not a cuddlebug, nor am I a snugglegrub –

but yes, we all need creature contact
in a safe consenting context
to engage in creature antics
far from thoughts of sin and syntax
but without a sexual subtext

don't we?

we all need gentle jostling, and snuggling and nuzzling
and any voice that says we don't – I think that voice needs muzzling
but because it's so embarrassing the benefit's debatable
I'd rather people thought I was at home with an inflatable
(than at a Cuddle Party in pyjamas)

I admire those who attend them for the humble path they've chosen
that of touchy-feely fellowship – it's called the road less frozen

they're just saying, "Don't ignore me, I am hurting. Please unthaw me."
I'm just saying, "I'm unthertain. Pleathe don't call me."

*There really are such things apparently.

IF I SAID YOU HAD A BIT OF A PROBLEM
WOULD YOU HOLD IT AGAINST ME?

alcohol – it's magical – it works its hocus pocus
makes all of us attractive, turns the shy ones into jokers

it's the precipice poured from a bottle
the gateway to heaven and hell
it's the portal that leads to a chortle
and a few other places as well

but while it makes the sour sweet, it turns the sweet things sour
and ask yourself who's really smiling during Happy Hour?

because there's
hinge-drinking – oils the social levers, eases you out of your shell
binge-drinking – leaves the shell well behind, heaves you out of your
                                                            skull
whinge-drinking – downing measures of wine as you outline your
                                                piteous condition
cringe-drinking – throwing out the baby of dignity with the
bathwater of inhibition

is one of these you?

don't be like the sopping wet pharaoh who said with a smile
"I just like a drink. I am not in denial..."

it's a soft, slow slide down a slippery slope
and no, you can't have ice with that
I mean the sort of slope it'll take twelve long, hard steps to climb
                                                            back up

sometimes the Path of Least Resistance
leads to the Place of Least Existence

don't let excessive moderation grind you down
but think
         before you drink
                  before you drown

NOT TONIGHT DEAR, I HAVE A BLACKBERRY

Your perky pocket PA winks and bleeps.
You take it to the loo to check your mail
 – the hand-held power hub that never sleeps –
stay too long, come back sweaty, glass-eyed, pale.

But in control. You've learnt to delegate,
keep cyber tabs on things, bring far to near,
send 'spin' memos to every wobbling plate,
become the wireless master puppeteer.

You're never, now, not ever, quite *away*.
Unthinkable to turn it off – and churlish.
Your status slips from puppeteer to prey,
the gizmo's got you by the late and earlies.

You are unfailingly available.
Resistance is feudal. You are in thrall,
have lost rights that were once inalienable,
are at its beck, buzz, flash, wink, beep and call.

Back to the bathroom, brush, wee, wash, click, wipe,
then sit unblinking, semi-catatonic,
in your online CA meeting, and type:
"Hi. My name's Matthew. I'm a cyberholic."

DON'T ASK

It's not just what I did, it's who I was.
Unemployed? Too small a word. I am Bereft.
I've gone from worker bee – the bee that does –
to true victim of identity theft.

Restored to stem cell status, a blank slate lent
both poignancy by what has been erased,
and urgency by my latest bank statement.
A wage-slave freed, disoriented, displaced –

and freed unasked, by over-generous masters.
A battery hen compelled to go free range.
They've been and gone and stitched me up, the bastards –
turned me into a strangely self-estranged

creased denizen of the involuntary sector –
thumb-twiddler, bird-feeder, library-lurker,
Lord of the Lounge, the remote my orb and sceptre,
Sudoku black belt, 'yes-but-that's-not-work'er

who'll grab at any hand that might reward me,
give me a brand and say, "You're part of us",
who craves a corporate Borg who will absorb me.
So, no – don't ask – I am not Spartacus...

BALLAD OF THE TROPICAL
SYSTEMATIC BOTANIST

he's a plucker, he's a picker
he's a cutter, he's a snipper
he knows too much about ginger and when given room to roam
he gathers great big armfuls of brand new botanic samples
and he presses them and logs them and he brings them all back
home

it's the only form of logging ecologically acceptable
he doesn't care if each new leaf's disgusting or delectable
toxic, psychotropic, soporific or medicinal
his quest is non-judgemental and completely unconditional

when he turns over a new leaf it's always pretty literal
"Ooh, not seen that one before…"

with his eyes on the horizon and his hand around a rhizome
you'll see him bleed but you won't hear him moan
with his ankles cut by switchgrass, far from home and Alan
Titchmarsh
he's a foliage-focused Indiana Jones

yeah he's a mild-mannered tropical systematic botanist
    but at the end of the day
he's a pretty determined-looking mild-mannered tropical systematic
botanist
    so don't get in his way

THE PRUNE STONE ORACLE

for practical career prognostication

TINKER

TAILOR

SOLDIER

SAILOR

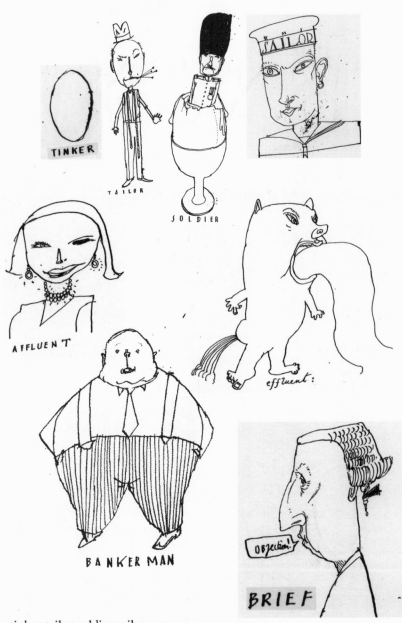

tinker, tailor, soldier, sailor
affluent, effluent, banker man, brief

drinker, abstainer, personal trainer
rich man, pure man, beauty, beast
actor, voyeur, pagan priest

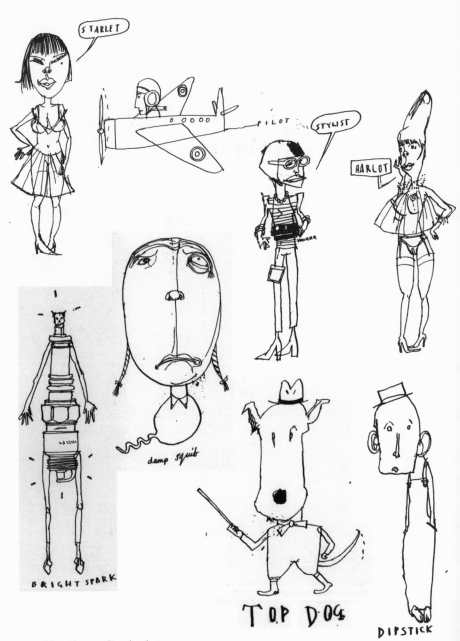

starlet, pilot, stylist, harlot
bright spark, damp squib, top dog, dipstick

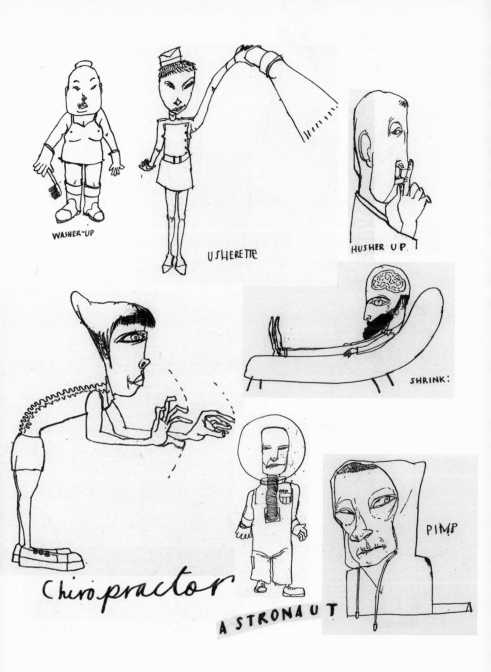

washer-up, usherette, husher-up, shrink
chiropractor, astronaut, pimp

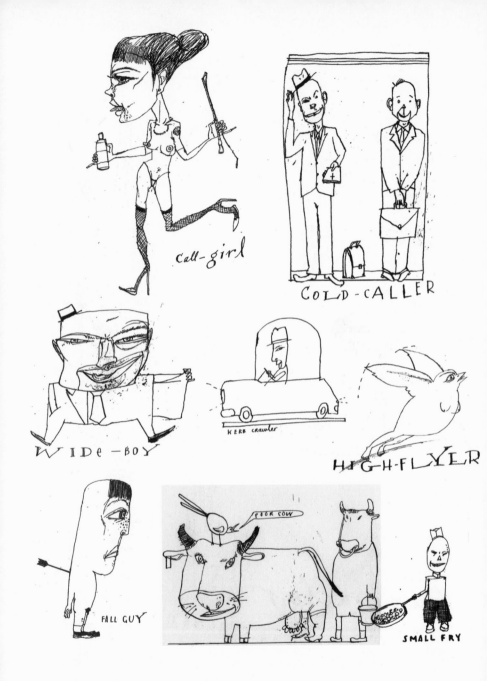

call-girl, cold-caller, wide-boy, kerb-crawler
high-flyer, fall guy, poor cow, small fry

brick-layer, soothsayer, darts player, social worker
statistician, dietician, fat controller

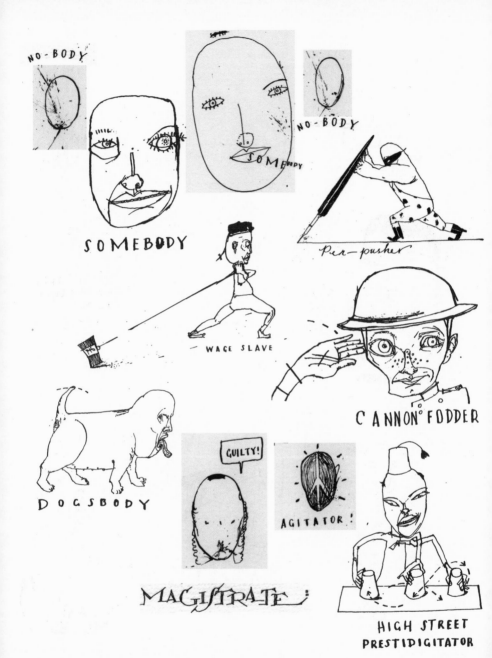

nobody, somebody, somebody, nobody
pen-pusher, wage-slave, cannon-fodder, dogsbody
magistrate, agitator, high-street prestidigitator

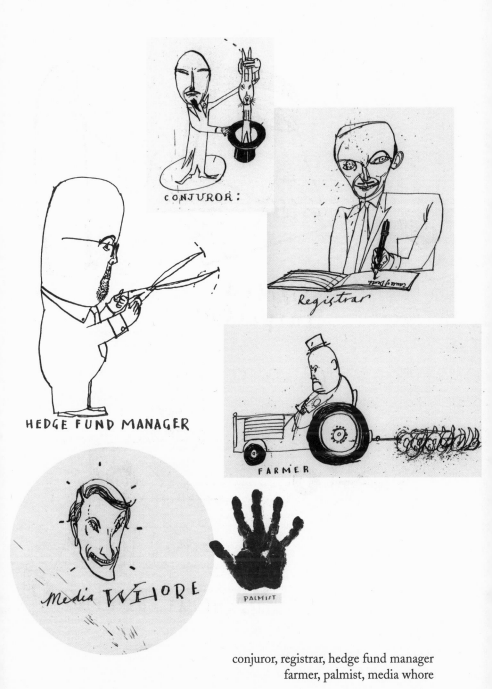

conjuror, registrar, hedge fund manager
farmer, palmist, media whore

Ofsted
inspector

Elvis Impersonator.

OFF-WHITE VAN MAN

·FUNERAL DIRECTOR·

Elvis impersonator, Ofsted inspector
off-white van man, funeral director

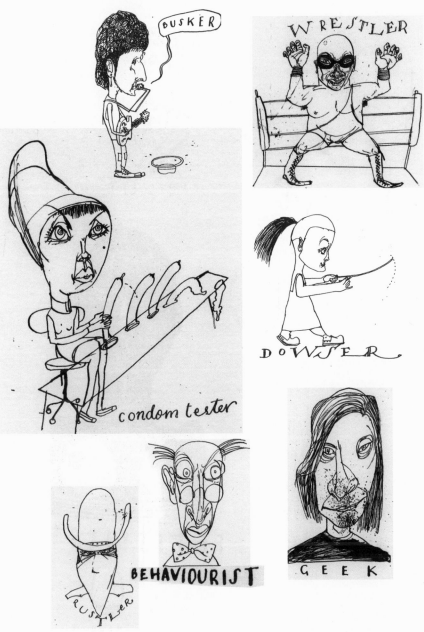

busker, wrestler, condom tester
dowser, rustler, behaviourist, geek

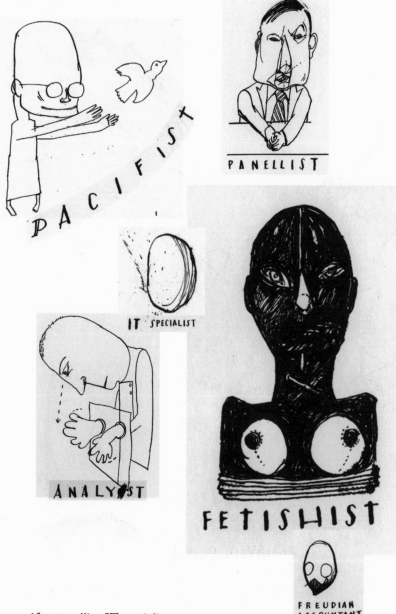

pacifist, panellist, IT specialist
analyst, fetishist, Freudian accountant

- BUTLER -

- BOUNCER -

Burglar

MINDER

ORGAN-GRINDER

Monkey TRAINER

butler, bouncer, burglar, minder
monkey-trainer, organ-grinder

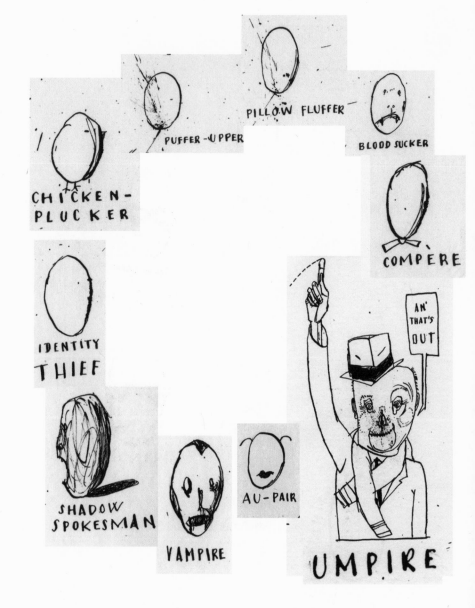

chicken-plucker, puffer-upper, pillow fluffer, blood-sucker
compère, umpire, au pair, vampire
shadow spokesman, identity thief

doctor
lawyer
Indian chief

WHERE EARWIGS DARE

A silver trail across the monitor;
fresh mouse-droppings beneath the swivel-chair;
the view obscured by rogue japonica.
Released into the wild, where earwigs dare –

you first went freelance – and then gently feral.
You worked from home – then wandered out again,
roughed it with spider, ant, shrew, blackbird, squirrel
in your own realm, your micro-Vatican.

No name conveys exactly what it is –
Chalet? Gazebo? You were not misled
by studios, snugs, garden offices,
workshops or outhouses. A shed's a shed –

and proud of it. You wouldn't want to hide it.
Wi-Fi-enabled rain-proof wooden box –
a box to sit in while you think outside it.
Self-rattling cage, den, poop-deck, paradox,

hutch with home-rule, cramped cubicle of freedom,
laboratory, thought-palace, bodger's bower,
plot both to sow seeds and to go to seed in,
cobwebbed, Cuprinol-scented, Seat of Power.

HOME

a place to consider the magic
a place to consider the world
to let my thought-forms hibernate
to see which way things will unfold

a place to imagine the Universe
a bolt-hole to practise the arts
a palace of generous living
that's more than the sum of its parts

a place to be true to my feelings
a place to be simple and calm
a neat nook or cranny or hideaway
to be perfectly safe from all harm

a nice bit of land in the country
a place to be close to the earth
a home with a heart and a hearthstone
to build up a new sense of worth

a cottage that's perched on a hillside
a flat in an old part of town
a place to fly high as a heart-string
a place to dig all the way down

a place to expand in the morning
to the sound of the songs of the birds
a place for a soul to be born in
somewhere to be free from all words

a place to be simple as sandbags
some place where enough is enough
a place to be happy as hi-fis
a place to be true to my love

a place to be thoroughly silly
a place to be wild as a wimp
or as still as a storm in a stethoscope
a place to be shrill as a shrimp

a place to be snug as a sandwich
to be extraordinarily odd
where to be quite naked is normal
a place to get close to my God

and to touch my invisible secret
a place where a whisper's a shout
a place to give strength to my seedling
a place to breathe in and breathe out

BREAD

I love the fresh-baked taste of you
the sandwiches I make of you

if you go stale, my love won't fail

I'll always see the good in you
the bread and butter pudding too

the breadcrumbs round the grateful fish
the soup-soaked croutons in the dish

if you go hard I'll keep the trust
and not discard a single crust

for you're the partner I have chosen
you make perfect toast from frozen

by crust and crumbs I pledge my troth
I'll always, always use my loaf

PRESENT TENSE

Round where I live there's a lot of pressure to live in the present. It's supposed to be good for you. People sometimes stop me in the street and say, "Hey Matt – be here now!" It's really irritating. I'm not convinced it's such a good thing, to live perpetually in the present. Now and again, sure. But always?

To explore this issue I've done a survey – not a scientific survey, just asking friends, family, people I meet, "Do you live in the present?" The results are intriguing.

There's quite a large group of people whose response to the question "Do you live in the present?" is "No – but I used to." They seem to experience a nostalgia for the present that's both poignant and paradoxical.

Another smaller group, faced with the question "Do you live in the present?" say, "No – but I will. I will." These people have put the present on a pedestal, and their very striving to get here makes it harder to reach.

A third, even smaller group, respond to the question "Do you live in the present?" with "Ah – would that I did…" I actually had to look these people up in a grammar book. It turns out they're living in the subjunctive. They're not easy people to make contact with or relate to, but it's worth making the effort. I sometimes think there ought to be special benefits available for such people – they ought to be able to claim Uncertainty Benefit, for example. But I can see how making that claim would be inherently problematic.

LESS IS MORE

can less be more, can more be less?
well, yes and no, and no and yes
well, more or less...

more bikes, fewer cars
less haze, more stars

less haste, more time
less reason, more rhyme

more time, less stress
fewer miles, more fresh (vegetables)

fewer car parks, more acres of available urban soil
more farmers' markets, less produce effectively marinated in crude oil

less colouring, more taste
more mashing, less waste

fewer couch potatoes, more spring greens
fewer tired tomatoes, more runner beans

more community, less isolation
less just sitting there, *more participation!*

more stillness, less inertia
less illness, more Echinacea

more wells (not oil ones, obviously), fewer ills
fewer clean fingernails, more skills

more co-operation, less compliancy
less complacency, more self-reliancy

less competition, more collaboration
less passive listening, *more participation!*

less attention defic…, more concentration
less passive listening, *more participation!*

(less repetition)

less of a warm globe, more of a chilly 'un
more of a wise world, fewer parts of CO_2 per million

less stress-related cardiovascular and pulmonary failure
more nurturing quality time in the company of a favourite clematis
    or dahlia

more craftsmanship, less built-in obsolescence
more political maturity, less apparently-consequence-free extended
    adolescence

more believed-to-be-beautiful, known-to-be-useful *things*
less cheap, pointless, petroleum-steeped *stuff*

so *Yes*, less *is* more – and enough's enough

KIPPERS FOR LIFE

you can serve yourself a kipper on a tasteful brekky platter
with a little bit of pepper it's the perfect kind of tucker
you can mash it in a pâté you can serve with toast and butter

put a little bit of kipper on the corner of a cracker
you can call it kipper canapés
Mmmmmmm

but should you come a cropper, slip or trip and drop your kipper –
there's no need to agonise about the kipper's injury
mix it up with egg 'n' rice and call it kipper kedgeree

it's got such versatility – DHA oil, omega 3,
there's calcium, and iodine, it lowers your cholesterol
in parts of middle England you can use them as collateral
apparently

a kipper in a jiffy bag can liven up a postal strike
or pop one in the pannier of a diplomatic motorbike

if you're feeling moody
you can happy-slap a foody

lying there like leatherwear, eyes glazed like a teddy bear
familiar, yet foreign, like a smooth, flat, smelly sporran

when they hang like golden ladies they're like aromatic bunting
they can lay false trails for hounds so you can sabotage the hunting
(which is where the term 'red herring' originates I'm told)

they enrich the English language and they're quite nice in a sandwich

so let's get a bumper sticker that will stick up for the kipper
and say, "A kipper is for life – not just for breakfast"

ON THE TENDENCY TOWARD GENDER STEREOTYPING AMONG HOMEWORKERS

They rise together, woken by the kids.
She feeds, wipes, wraps and zips them in to school.
     He turns his laptop on, and focuses.
She launders, shops, brings home formidable
stocks, stacks them, puts a pan on low, completes
a tax form, phones them up, is put on hold…
     He types a line, deletes, types, re-deletes.
She stirs. Her mobile goes. Yvette's been told
she's obsolete, redundant. Oh, how awful!
She's taken off hold. Yvette starts to cry.
The unwatched pan boils over. There's the doorbell.
She pushes his door, taps to catch his eye.
     He looks up crossly at third time of asking:
     Don't interrupt me when I'm mono-tasking!

WILFRED FROM ILFORD

Wilfred from Ilford pilfers things:
clothing, food, watches, rings -
any type of stuff he'll swipe.
But the fact is, in spite of all the practice
Wilf puts in, he isn't very good at it.
He's more Wilful than skilful
and not being the sort
to consider the consequences of his actions
he gets caught a lot and put in prison
or on probation (depending on
how many other offences he's asked
to be taken into consideration).
His friends say, "What
is it with you, Wilf,
that you have to pilf-
er all this stuff?
You have enough
to live on, it's not
as if you're ill-fed in Ilford, Wilfred, is it?
We're fed up having to visit you in gaol.
Why do you do it, Wilf? Why?
Why put yourself beyond the pale?"
The truth is, Wilfred is not a well man.
He doesn't steal for personal gain
but to ease an ongoing pain.
Consumed with anxiety about the state of society,
steeped in regret about Third World Debt,
Wilf lies awake at night, worrying
about famine abroad and homelessness at home.
Tossing and turning in his bed
he's conscious of rainforests burning
and the unburied dead
of wars being fought as he tries to sleep
dig deep into his psyche.

As he ponders the way
the world's resources are squandered
and wonders if humankind has blundered
once too often and plundered
more than can ever be repaid,
he is dismayed, and seeks inside himself
the solution to pollution, the answer to cancer,
the key to free us all from inequality.
As a chap who feels the gap
between rich and poor
to be his personal concern, he can't turn
a blind eye or shut the door
on other people's suffering.
And it's to take his mind off it
that Wilfred steals – not for profit.
While the rest of us shrug and shake our heads
and shiftily avert our gaze,
Wilfred will take all the problems of the world on his shoulders.
And walk off with them.

THE NEITHER HERE OR THERE MAN

the neither here or there man
is neither there nor here
he's the not-quite-anywhere-man
he's neither far nor near

he's semi-inconsistent
the way he gets about
his absence is persistent
his presence is in doubt

some say it isn't normal
and doesn't make much sense
they find it too informal –
they're inclined to take offence:

Why can't you exist properly?
look – other people can
you *are* so very sloppily
you under-present man

it's not too much to ask, really
to be either here or there
and to be so quite sincerely
it's really only fair

it's really only natural
and not hard to understand
that we ask you to be actual
and firm beneath the hand

but the neither here nor there man
says neither yes nor no
he's a not-a-lot-to-spare man
with nowhere else to go

and I venture the suggestion
that the problem isn't his
he causes no congestion
it's enough he simply is

UPTURN FOR THE TURNIP

sales of turnips are up 100%

it's the upside of the down-turn
it's a turn-up for the turnip,
its neep tide has turned
and we've learned not to spurn it

they stretch out a stew
and they bulk up a casserole
so now Baldrick's brassica's
back in our dinner-bowl

nijamiegordeliawhittingrhodes
all endorse and explain how to fashion it
I have seen the post-credit-crunch future-munch
and it's got mash in it

SUPERMARKET

The black-and-yellow metal arm
does simple semaphore,
admitting shuttlebugs
– portable private spaces –
from out of which pile people,
half-dazed delegates from double-glazed caves
briefed to fill fridge-freezers, flush fitted units
and flat Formica surfaces.

A continuous consumer wave of punter-gatherers
each personable particle charged with purchasing power
they swarm from one warm world into another
towards the automatic doors whose Perspex jaws
slide open greedily once their purpose is assured –
into a world of bread smells, mixed vegetables
and instant mashed metaphors.

In they pour, through the maw
of the fabulous flesh-eating flower,
drone in in droves to browse,
drowsily, its sticky aisles –
help themselves to cut-price pollen
and knock-down nectar from its shelves.

Then they proffer plastic loyalty
and credit-card credentials,
till the I Ching! of the till says: No Blame
and laden with luxurious essentials
the spent particles emerge
into the 3D grid – the two-acre database –
where their multichrome homes-from-home
wait, immaculate, slotted
between allotted lines
like shiny concepts in a tidy mind.

LET THEM SPEAK LATIN

I often say, "quidquid latine dictum sit altum videtur"
but when I say it I say it quite wryly
because it means "whatever is written in Latin is looked upon highly"
and since Latin's been superseded as the lingua franca
speaking it means you come across as a bit of a classicist

although a lover of Latin may not be a Latin lover
I don't think you should judge a Latin scholar by his cover

we all speak a bit of Latin and it's time that we admitted it
if Latin's an offence then let's face it we've committed it –
modus vivendi is still pretty trendy
modus operandi can still come in handy – and vice versa

who hasn't been caught in flagrante delicto
a bit of Latin on their lips, sucking on its big toe (as it were)
saying subpoena, habeas corpus, alter ego or agenda
bona fide, terra firma, innuendo or pudenda?

if even ergo's in your argot, ipso facto, you speak Latin
     and that's fine
so if you're offered Latin lessons, don't feel you must decline
because it isn't all amo-ing and amas-ing and amat-ing
     is Latin
I feel a tad defensive about its cases and its tenses:
the nominative, the ablative, the dative, the accusative
the tentative, the putative, the sensitive, the fugitive

and far be it from me to propagate unproven claims
but a lot of plants would die if we forgot their Latin names

Latin's not a dead language – although it could be more animated
it hasn't been embalmed as such, just a little laminated
so I say to Latin lovers everywhere, you mark my memorandum:
nil illegitimi carborundum and quod erat demonstrandum

PS Dulce et decorum est to get these feelings off my chest

WORKS PERKS

...it's just a little thing,
I wouldn't call it pilfering
or petty theft. I took one, yes
but look – there are so many left.
I'm in on time. I smile, work hard.
Why should my conscience twitch or flinch?
Each working week you take a yard,
so why begrudge me my half-inch?

You take the best hours of my day
what do you give me? Take-home pay.
I'm so tired I can hardly speak
you take the best days of my week.
You take the best weeks of my month
I take some paper, this hole-punch.
You take the best months of my year
I take this swivel-chair. Oh dear.
You take the best years of my life...
...a laminator for the wife.

So now please look the other way –
I need my little takeaway
to give myself a token raise
to supplement my take-home praise.

Some get to meet celebrities
or go on junkets overseas
I'm simply taking some of these –
some paper clips, some folder files
a Pritt Stick, stapler, carpet tiles
some Tipp-Ex, a waste-paper bin
this *thing* for putting *thingies* in
this ream. Okay this box of reams
this laptop...
...well, you took my *dreams*.

How did ever come to this?
My perky chirpy perquisites
have been turned into exhibits –
these trinkets I gave house-room to:
Exhibits 'A' to 'W'.

Don't ask what reason or what rhyme
drove pretty me to petty crime
nobody's perfect
I guess it built up over time
because I'm worth it.

HO BLOODY HO

You don't have to be mad to work here and
we're not. Just tired. Jaded. But still we go
and stand in clumps, a drink in every hand,
a safe way from the hopeless mistletoe.
The new girl looks alarmed – surprised she came
given the tales we tell about last year.

"The photocopier's never been the same."
Dawn acts as chaperone and bends her ear.
"Watch out for George, Debs." "Why?" "Thinks he's a poet."
Debs smiles obligingly and looks confused.
Later her drinking borders on heroic.
She's all right, her. Look, see how soon the booze

has softened, smudged, fudged, eased tongues off the leash,
glazed shiny faces in vague bonhomie.
Bob 'BossMan' Jephson makes his annual speech
concluding: "We're just one big family…"
"…Please," Dawn stage whispers, "Take me into care."
Jo Watlington snorts Pernod through her nose.
The BossMan beams, and leaves by the back stair.
Mim Corbett tells her joke. A toast's proposed.

There's even warmth in the traditional groan
That greets George as he shapes to read his poem:

Don't give me bah humbug – I'm not playing Scrooge
Don't wince at my tinsel – I'm not in the mood
No man is an island – No woman is an isthmus
And people are people wherever you go
So have a Merry Christhmus…

MIND THE GAP

I'm hardly anything, but I go on almost forever
people on the whole hardly ever, ever
pay me any mind
but everyone knows I'm there
if they care to care to notice
because I'm the gap
I'm the yawning gap, the awesome gap
the tragic magic slapstick gap
the gap between the map
    and the territory
between the tabloid rap
    and the real story
the charming chap
    and the sleazy Tory
the revelation gap
the emanation gap
the generation gap
the hesitation gap
I'm the strange elusive space between
what people say – and what we mean
what's really there – and what is seen
between the sense of duty – and the secret dream
between the outward calm – and the inward scream
    I'm the exact difference
    I'm the distance between
so please, if you could,
shortly after the end of the poem
but before you start to clap
spare a thought for me
and Mind the Gap

CLIENT OF THE YEAR

My psychotherapy is going very well, thank you for wondering. I know it's going well, not just in itself, but also in comparison with other people's therapeutic journeys. It's not always easy to know how you're doing in relation to others. Counsellors and psychotherapists have their conferences, where they can discuss the latest fads and theories and compare case histories. The clients meanwhile are just supposed to sit at home and fret, perhaps brood a little. Recently, however, my therapist asked if he could enter me into the Client of the Year Show, in Earl's Court.

My first reaction, to be honest, was to feel flattered. Only then did I think: I'm not sure this is strictly ethical. But my therapist told me that if I was willing to go in for it he'd give me a 15% reduction in fees, plus he'd take off his Sony Walkman. This had become a bit of an issue between us, and I thought it's a good deal, let's just go for it.

I did well, too. I was entered into the Jungian section, in the Thinking/Sensation category, and I won a rosette for Best of Type. It was fantastic, very affirming. I think I'd have done better overall, too, but I got so excited I bit one of the judges.

My feeling at the time was that their attitude to this understandable faux pas was very judgemental, but when I worked on it later my therapist pointed out that they were, basically, judges. I found this a very helpful perspective from which to come to terms with their behaviour.

The competition as a whole was won by a woman who'd been working with a Gestalt Therapist. It was controversial, because although she won the competition fair and square, a part of her came in third, and yet another part of her wasn't even placed. There'd been further controversy when a coach-load of Co-Counsellors who'd come down from Coventry tried to enter each other into the Client of the Year Show, but were deemed ineligible and disqualified.

They hotly disputed this ruling and, unwilling to leave without making a point, staged a protest outside the auditorium – carrying banners that said things LIKE THIS BRINGS UP FEELINGS OF HURT, REJECTION AND SOME ANGER. This protest triggered a counter-demonstration by Person-Centred Rogerian Counsellors, who carried banners saying HMMMM, and even, from some of the more militant ones, WOULD YOU LIKE TO EXPLORE THIS FURTHER?

WONDERMENTAL THINGS

the wondermental things apply
as quirky quantum time goes by

it's quirky *and* it's quarky
and it's kind of like a doorkey
to a world so charmed and murky
only physicists can visit it
and handle its vicissitudes

it is a most absorbing thing
to watch electrons orbiting
to sit there and imagine them
without a hope of catching them

the fundamental particles
least definite of articles

though smaller than bacteria
they're in no way inferior
they occupy less area
are infinitely eerier
and scarier

so much that even physicists
can hardly grasp that they exist

they have 'non-local' properties
exist as probabilities
as possibles and parallels
as parables and dizzy spells

a neo-nano-nothingness
attention-seeking emptiness
an absence with an aftertaste
a ripple in a state of grace

for some the subatomic's
both a riddle and a tonic

east of reason, shy of rhyme
the quantum world confirms that time
is circular and cyclical

on top of that it speaks of why
the wondermental things apply
as quarky quantum time goes by

LIFE IS SO MUCH EASIER WITH EFFECTIVE ANALGESIA

if the purpose of pain is to say to the brain:
Ow! Houston we have a problem...
then once we've got the message we don't need it again and again. . .

[Chorus*] What do we want?   Symptom relief!
*   When do we want it?   Now!*

when you've had enough of it there's just no need to suffer it
pop a little caplet and Ibuprofen will buffer it

I've had a go with Aspirin, Codeine and Paracetamol
with Solpadeine, Co-codamol, with Anadin and Ultramol
I love them all, I really do, but I prefer Ibuprofen

there are other non-steroidal anti-inflammatory drugs around
your NSAIDs these days are quite thick on the ground
there's Naproxen, there's Nabumetone
    and, of course, there's Indomethacin
each with much to offer us. But I prefer Ibuprofen

I love the way the compound sticks its cheeky little hand in
the way it blocks the enzyme that creates the prostaglandin
reducing fever, inflammation, and mild to moderate pain

yes I know it isn't curative, in any way preventative
but to dwell on what it doesn't do is anally retentative

I know it doesn't treat the cause, the cause will still be there
but it lends a hand, it puts the 'pal' back into palliative care.
it does exactly what you'd expect it to say it would do if it came in a tin

* *[Insert chorus at will]*

FLY

I take a friendly interest in the fly
that buzzes round me as I sit and write.
Phlegmatic fly, I wonder what there might
be going on in you. I'd like to pry
inside your little exo-skeleton
and look out from behind your compound eyes.
Perhaps we would be in for a surprise,
and you might not be quite the simpleton
that we have long assumed from outward signs,
but possessed of a vast intelligence
whose breadth and scope our minds could never guess.
We plod along the same familiar lines,
and can't make much variety of sense.
Perhaps you make far more. Or slightly less.

CHARGE OF THE LATE BRIGADE

with apologies and pitiful excuses to Alfred Lord Tennyson

Half an hour, half an hour
  Half an hour wrongward
Flustered and out of breath
  Drive the unnumbered
Forward the Late Brigade
Leaving their beds unmade
Fretful and out of breath
  Drive the unslumbered

Hungover, pounding head
Dredge themselves out of bed
Traffic lights turn to red
  Feather their clutches
Theirs not to make excuse,
Edit or twist the truth,
Give it some extra juice,
Into the realm of statistics
  Drive the unpunctual

Unknowns to right of them
What ifs to left of them
If onlys behind them
  Whispered and muttered
If they'd not drunk so much
Used Merlot as a crutch
Into a state of dread
Into a state of funk
  Sink the tut-tutted

Merciless seconds tick
Mercenary minutes tock
Tock round a spinning clock
Spin till their head is sick
    Sick with exhaustion
Swimming with dread and doubt
Will colleagues scowl and pout

Worse will they swear and shout
Shout "three strikes and you're out!"
    Issue a caution?
Easy to get it out
    Of all proportion

When will their story fade?
Each working day it's played
    Same tune unbroken
Humour the charge they made
Humour the Late Brigade
"Of course you were delayed
    Now get some work done"

E-SONNET

Daily diaspora of signals, neural
sparks, paperless clutter, fact-opinion.
I am viral, extra-mural. I am plural.
I'm the 'e' in evolution. I'm Darwinian.
I'm the encroacher. I'm the great Instead:
of letters, notes, talk, postcards, memos, syntax –
the phisher-king preying on the easily led
the spam that seeks to fertilise your inbox.
I am the information superhighwayman
demand your time with subtle menaces
and blandishments to tempt you to reply to them –
exemplary parthenogenesis.
I breed, though I am neither male nor female.
I'm victorious. I am legion. I am email.

BOTOX

early onset
taxidermy

ONWARD CITY MOMENTS

onward city moments
    with your all-concerning paths
your disconcerting crime rate
    and your public swimming baths

with your traffic flowing slower
    than your gutters and your drains
with your concrete, your congestion
    and your stubborn understains

onward city moments
    with your teeming seedy charm
your naked neon nightspots
    and your early morning calm

onward city slickers
    in your fashionable clothes
with your humorous car stickers
    and your hokey-cokey nose

onward city monuments
    I bow my humble head
before your effigies in tribute
    to your high-achieving dead

I praise the public servants
    who keep your channels clean
and lubricate the moving parts
    of your obese machine

onward city moments
    ever onward on your way
with your cast of motley millions
    pulling through another day

BY 5PM TUESDAY

A deadline has a silent 'r'.
It is a navigable star –
a beckoning that leads to a reckoning.
It's a line in the sand
drawn by the arbitrary hand
of whim and circumstance.

Great for getting things done
while killing any fun
you might have had doing it.

It's a mardy Mr Motivator,
a tart galvanic vinegar,
a rallying point for the wasps of anxiety.

A deadline awakens in the procrastinator
what they most fear and long for –
the coming of the Anti Crastinator.

It is the brawny Fairy Godmother
who drags Deep Sea Cinderella to the surface
where she swells to Ugly Sister proportions,
bursts her glass slippers, meets her Prince Charming
and hands him an invoice.

It is the pragmatic power that pulls the poem
from the Platonic realm of possibility
to awkward earth where its perfect potential
shall be sullied and diminished.

But at least it's finished.